THE MADAD

Restoring Ancient Landmarks

2015

Shelem Ministry Presents Part II:

THE MADAD

Restoring Ancient Landmarks

Yibniyah Hawkins Chief Executive Counsellor
Shelem Ministry
7/15/2015

The Madad Restoring the Ancient Landmarks.

Published by Shelem Ministry

Contract|www.shelemministry@yahoo.com

325.320.4327 |www.shelemministry.org

Shelem Ministry acting in the auxiliary role as a ministerial organization for world peace has as its core mission to introduce to all nations "The Ephah™". The Ephah™ is a body of standards (just measures) for establishing lasting peace. The Ephah™ is designed to give official guidance and direction for resolving all issues regarding community, domestic, foreign, and international issues we face today.

The Ephah™ will introduce an approved model for true government. It is designed to serve as a basis of comparison to which the excellence and correctness of all issues, circumstances and problems may be determined. The name Shelem conveys by its meaning the ideal condition of perfect peace. The "Zevach Shelem" the peace offering is ordained by Yahweh so as to unite the religious worship with the enjoyment of domestic, national, and international peace is a voluntary offering to bring peace between opposing individuals and nations. The offering of peace will also estore an alliance based on friendship, love for your fellowman, and a love for peace.

Shelem Ministry will also be a motivating force in establishing a state of moral inspiration by teaching the morals inherently embodied within the Laws of Peace and the Ephah™. The Ephah™ will introduce to the nations and people alike 20 foundational laws instructing them concerning their moral obligation to the earth and their fellowman.

Scripture quotation mark "KJV" are taken from the "PNV-KJV" are taken from the Proper Name Version of the King James Bible Copyrighted 2010. LRI Publishers U.S.A. Used by permission all rights reserved.

The Madad

Restoring the Ancient Landmarks

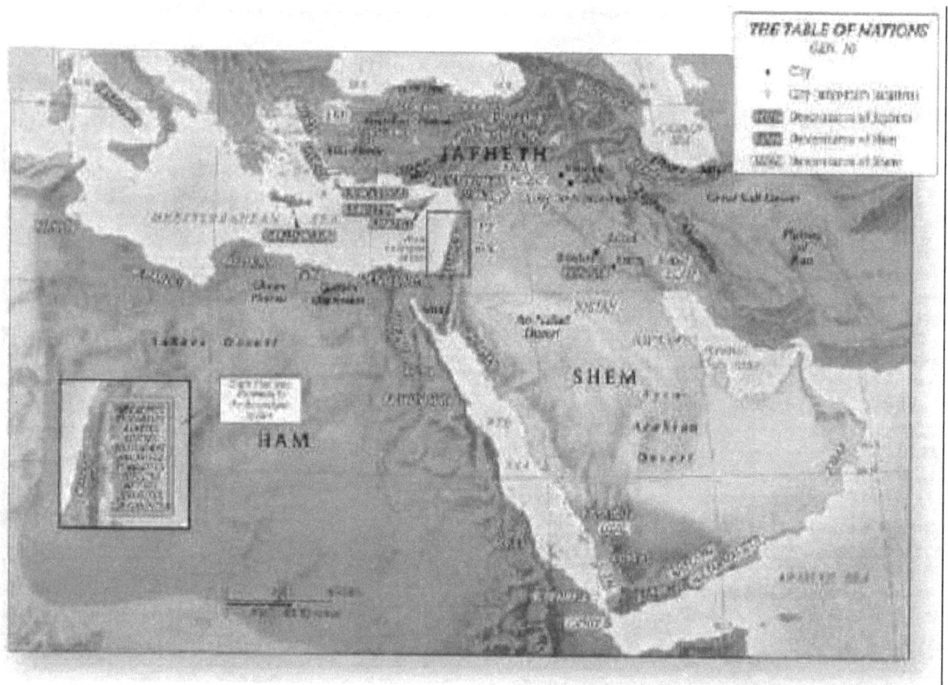

He has cast the lot for them, and his hand has divided it among them with a measure line. They shall possess it forever, from generation to generation shall they dwell therein.

Isaiah 34:17 (KJV)

This work will be a continuation of the original work entitle the Madad Restoring the Ancient Landmarks that we presented to the nations. We will address the United Nations Security Council Resolution 242 adopted on November 22, 1967. This resolution has survived the times sense it commencement and served as the basis of many peace initiatives present by the United Nations in regards to the Israeli and Palestinian conflict. The United Nations Security Council Resolution 242 is based on the principles outline in United Nations Charter regarding the "inadmissibility of the acquisition of territory by war". This principle also implores all nations to work for just and lasting peace in the Middle East.

This principle is just but it has an element of remissness in regard to reversing past violation of its core essence. The core essence of this principle which states the acquisition of territory with the spirit of conquest, greed and injustice resulting from war violates a essential right establish from the beginning for all nations and people alike and this is the "right of inheritance". This principle of the United Nations charter must be "retroactive" to a prior time in regards to the land of Israel were a people were forced by war to evacuated their land while other nations in succession have occupied their land by force.

This land by "Writ of sequestration" has remain under the control of the nations and not return to the original people who received it by inheritance. This Writ of sequestration was to remain in place until the

Hebrew people complied with their covenantal obligations and pay for their sins. The invading of the land permitted by Yahweh was to only give limited Trusteeship to the nations who he foreknew would occupy the inherited land of Israel. The principle outlined in the United Nation Charter in regards to the inadmissibility of acquisition of territory by war is the basis on which the prophetic injunction to sequester the land of Israel under the control of several nations.

And I will bring upon that land all my words which I have pronounced against it, *even* all that is written in this book, which Jeremiah has prophesied against all the nations. For many nations and great kings shall make slaves of them also: and I will recompense them according to their deeds, and according to the works of their own hands.

Jeremiah 25:13-14 (KJV)

And command them to say unto their rulers, This what Yahweh of Host, the Father of Israel says; This you must say unto your rulers; I have made the earth, the man and the beast that *are* upon the ground, by my great power and by my outstretched arm, and have given it unto whom it seemed best unto me. And now have I given all these lands into the *hand* of Nebuchadnezzar the king of Babylon, my servant; and the beasts of the field have I given him also to serve him. And all nations shall serve him, and his son, and his son's son, until a specified time has come: and *then many nations and great kings shall make slaves them also*.

Jeremiah 27:4-7 (KJV)

The word "hand" written in Jeremiah 27:6 is from the Hebrew word:

יָד yād : a primitive word; a *hand* (the *open* one [indicating *power, means, direction*; used (as noun, adverb, etc.) in a great variety of applications, both literal and figurative it means: a charge, creditor, custody, debt, dominion. Yad: (2i) *means giving something into one's hand is entrusting it to him under his power and rule* —Strong's Exhaustive Concordance of the Bible Red-Letter Edition by James Strong's

יָד yād: In a literal are restricted sense means, the hand: in the figurative and general sense, it is an executive force, dominion: it is every kind of aid, instrument work, **term**; and administration. The Hebrew Tongue Restored by Fabre de Olivet Part 1 page 362-363.

The word hand is revealing to us that Yahweh gave Trusteeship to the nations of Babylon, Media-Persia, Greece, Roman, Arab's and Islamic nations who by conquest occupied the land of Israel, but this was only to be for a time. The right of acquisition of the land of Israel was not given to either of these nations instead the original right of inheritance is preserved for the Hebrew/Israelites who rightful owned the land. Shelem Ministry implores the United Nations to retroactively apply the United Nations principle regarding the "inadmissibility of the acquisition of territory by war and conquest and reverse over three thousand years of injustice inflicted upon the children of Israel.

The acquisition of the land of Israel by several nations throughout history stands to test the validity and creditability of the United Nations principle to correct the injustice of nations who through policy perpetrated their colonialist ambition on other nations. Shelem Ministry is proposing a question that remains to be answer by the community of nation. The pervious occupations of the land of Israel known today as Palestine were these occupations the result of war and conquest? If the nations will answer this question honestly it is obvious the answer is yes. The nations are admonish in this generation to reverse the injustice inflicted upon a people who remain today exiled from their homeland. In the Madad a work to restore the ancient landmarks we revealed to the nations in the days of Noah this land was taken by force from its rightful owners.

 The original owners of the land of Palestine are known in the Holy Writ as the children of Abraham. This historical fact we have recorded for us in both the Holy Writ and secular history. The Holy Writ reveals this land was taken by force from the Hebrews by several nations who occupied it through war and have laid claim to it as their possession. The principle of inadmissibility of the acquisition of territory by war can through a process of **"retroactivity"** in this generation reverse the injustice inflicted upon the original Hebrew/Israelites who received this land as inheritance by an everlasting covenant of peace.

In Article 2 of the United Nation Charter it embodies the legal principle the no title or ownership of land could be establish by conquest. History reveals to us the land of Israel and much of the Arab lands have experience centuries of war and occupation by several nations. The history concerning the Muslim Conquest documents emphatically these conquest resulted in large swaths of land from India in the east to Spain in the west were conquered including the land of Israel.

The history concerning the Muslim Conquest is validated by both Muslim and Christian scholars. They all agree and make very clear in their works the Muslim Conquest resulted in the occupation of all the lands that is called today the Muslim world. The first major conquest is renowned for its brutality occurred in the Arabia immediately after the death of Muhammad in 632. This conquest is known in history as the "Ridda Wars or Apostasy Wars". History reveals that tens of thousands of Arabs vere put to death until their tribes re-submitted to Islam. Omar launched he next conquest in these conquests history reveals several nations were occupied by force.

- Syria was conquered around 636
- Egypt was conquered around 641
- Mesopotamia and the Persia Empire around 650
- In the early 8th century all of North Africa, Spain to the West, the lands of central Asia and India to the East were conquered.

The conquest of the nations who occupied the land of Israel were all the result of war. The Roman and Muslim conquest caused the original Hebrews who occupied the land to be exiled into Arabia and into the north, south and western regions of Africa causing them to be removed from their allotted inheritance. The United Nations cannot ignore the facts of history that many of the Arabs who occupy the land of Israel have claimed this land by conquest.

In 629 Palestine was invaded by Arabs from the Hejaz in 635 A.D. Palestine, Jordan, Syria and Jerusalem were in the Muslims hands. This was called in history the "Islamic Conquest of Palestine". This conquest resulted in the "Islamization of Palestine" in 640 A.D. This resulted in the migration of Muslim Arabs from other regions into Palestine. The migration of Arab Muslim into Palestine resulted in "acculturation" of the local inhabitants into Arab identity and Arabic became the official language.

The historian James William Parkes revealed in his work during the 1 century after the **"Arab Conquest"** (640-740) the Caliph and governors of Syria and the Holy Land ruled both the Christians and Hebrews.

In the 9th century Palestine was conquered by the Fatimid dynasty out of North Africa. The Byzantine Romans who ruled Palestine prior to this conquest attempted to regain their lost territories including Jerusalem from the Arabs. The Arab Muslim history in the region of Palestine began in 630 A.D in conjunction with the "Great Muslim Conquest". The presence of Arabs has continued to develop to this present time for about 1400 years. The lands allotted by inheritance to the children of Abraham by an everlasting covenant of peace has remain under foreign occupying powers until this day as prophesied. The foreign occupying powers of the lands allotted by covenant were all obtained by conquest and not by divine appointment.

In this generation the Kingdom of Jordon occupied and capture in 1948 Arab-Israeli war the Temple Mount and all of the West Bank. It is a historical fact that upon conquering the West Bank the Jordanians worked to remove all traces of Jordanian Arab identity by annexed the territory into Jordan. They planned to integrate the Arabs who lived their into the Jordan's social structure. In 1964 Palestinians in Jordan occupied East Jerusalem establishing at that time the Palestine Liberation Organization for the liberation of Jerusalem from the Zionist. The PLO was also establish to prevent the establishment of the State of Israel in the land belong to the Arabs. It is a fact prior to June 4, 1967 their never existed in the history of mankind a people called "Palestinians". The people who resided in the land we traditionally called Palestine were known throughout history as Arabs who are the children of Abraham.

There has never existed in the history of man a people called the "Palestinians" are a Palestinian culture, language or history. We do have evidence of an Arab people, culture, language and a history recorded for us. The Arab people who are the children of Abraham through Ishmael nd Keturah have a legitimate right to land allotted by inheritance to Abraham.

The United Nations has an opportunity in this generation to encourage and influence peace between the Israeli and Palestinians, but ultimately the establishing of lasting peace must be the result of negotiation between these two brothers. The negotiation between this two brothers must be based on the right of inheritance they both share in the allotted land appointed to their common ancestor Abraham by an everlasting covenant. The only way to end the years of conflict between this two ancient people is to "Restore the Ancient Landmarks establish by Yahweh in the days of Noah.

The United Nations must uphold at this time the principles and purpose outlined in its Charter that support the ancient statutes outline in Part 1 of "The Madad". These statutes are "just standards" for protecting and securing for all nations the right of inheritance. Notice these just standards recorded in the Holy Writ.

- **<u>Law#1</u>**: You shall not remove your neighbor's landmark, which they of old time have set in your inheritance, which you shall inherit in the land that Yahweh your Father gives you to possess.

   Deuteronomy 19:14 (KJV)

- Remove not the old landmark; and intrude not on the lands of the fatherless:

   Proverb 23:10 (KJV)

- Law # 2. Yahweh spoke to Moses, saying, to these the land shall be divided for an inheritance according to the number of names. To a larger tribe you shall give a larger inheritance, and to

smaller you shall give them a smaller inheritance: to every one shall his inheritance be given according to those that were numbered of him. **The land _(earth)_ shall be divided by lot:** according to the names of the tribes of their fathers they shall inherit. According to the lot shall the inheritance be divided between larger and smaller,
Numbers 26:52-56 (KJV)

- When Yahweh divided to the nations their inheritance, when he separated all of mankind, he set the boundary lines for the people according to the number of the children of Israel.
Deuteronomy 32:8 (KJV)

The just principles outline in these statutes are instructing the governments of mankind to not remove are intrude upon the lands of other nations. The above statutes describe prohibition against the acts of taking, and seizing by force, and also occupying a land in the place of the original inhabitants. The first law prohibits as the United Nations principle concerning the "inadmissibility of the acquisition of territory by war". The second law listed above commands the earth to be divided as an inheritance to all nations and the boundary lines and borders to establish within all nations. This law also commands that all people on earth should receive as an inheritance an allotted amount of land and this land should be protected by a universal law.

This law should establish and protect for all nations the right of inheritance in the lands they received by an everlasting covenant. There is a universal human right that we can never ignore and that is "everything on earth was created to be shared and the unique resources connected with the ownership of all the land on earth was given to all nations as an inheritance. This universal right also includes the right of all people to function freely in their unique place on earth without the fear of a state or a condition of being subjected to external rule or control. There should be universal laws agreed upon by all nations that would protect the rights of all nations in their individual inheritances securing the right to possess, enjoy and have secured to them a homeland. These laws must prohibit exploitation, extortion and the use of force to control the natural resources and wealth of another nation. The United Nations Charter which outlines its principles and purposes in the face of current events has not adhere to their principles fully in regards to the Israeli and Palestinians conflict. Notice the articles listed below that constituted the Charter of United Nations if this principles were adhere to they could reverse years of bloodshed and injustice that has existed in the Middle East.

CHAPTER I
PURPOSES AND PRINCIPLES
Article 1
The Purposes of the United Nations are:
1. To maintain international peace and security, and to that end: to take effective collective measures for the prevention and removal of threats to the peace, and for the suppression of acts of aggression or other breaches of the peace, _and to bring about by peaceful means, and in conformity with the principles of justice and international law, adjustment or_

2. To develop friendly relations among nations based on respect for the principle of equal rights and self-determination of peoples, and to take other appropriate measures to strengthen universal peace;

4. All Members shall refrain in their international relations from the threat or use of force against the territorial integrity or political independence of any state, or in any other manner inconsistent with the Purposes of the United Nations.

Article 13
1. The General Assembly shall initiate studies and make recommendations for the purpose of:

a. promoting international co-operation in the political field and encouraging the progressive development of international law and its codification;

b. promoting international co-operation in the economic, social, cultural, educational, and health fields, an assisting in the realization of human rights and fundamental freedoms for all without distinction as to race, sex, language, or religion.

Article 14
Subject to the provisions of Article 12, the General Assembly may recommend measures for the peaceful adjustment of any situation, regardless of origin, which it deems likely to impair the general welfare or friendly relations among nations, including situations resulting from a violation of the provisions of the present Charter setting forth the Purposes and Principles of the United Nations.

Notice in Articles 1 and 14 were the charter calls for United Nations to bring about peace by conforming to justice principles and international law and to make necessary adjustment for the settlement of international disputes or situation. Article 14 supports this fact by stating the General Assembly my recommend measures for the adjustment of any situation causing a breach in the establishment of peace regardless of its **"origin"** **which it deems to impair the general welfare and friendly relation among nations including situation resulting from a violation of the provision of the present Charter setting for the Purposes and Principle of the United Nations.**

These Article supports that point we are making all conquest regardless of their origin are not admissible for occupation of a land. Shelem Ministry in Part 1 of the Madad introduced to the nations the everlasting "Covenant of Peace" were Yahweh in the days of Noah allotted by this covenant all nations their inherited lands. This covenant secured to them the ownership of all things connected to the land and a perpetual right to occupy these land without fear of conquest. The sons of Noah Shem, Ham and Yahphet were all given their respectful inheritance with define boundary lines and borders. The historical evidence of children of Arphaxad and his descendants which includes Abraham were forceful evacuated from their inheritance. The first recorded conquest after the universal flood was carried out by Cush, Canaan and the other sons of Ham. This resulted in the first occupation of the land of Palestine by conquest by the Canaanites who occupy this land in violation of an oath. Then followed the Assyrians, Babylonians, Media-Persian, Greece,

Romans, and the Arab-Muslim who all occupied this land allotted by divine appointment to the children of Israel. Let's us continue to examine the principles and purpose of the United Nations Charter.

CHAPTER VI
PACIFIC SETTLEMENT OF DISPUTES
Article 33
1. The parties to any dispute, the continuance of which is likely to endanger the maintenance of international peace and security, shall, first seek *a solution by negotiation, enquiry, mediation, conciliation, arbitration, judicial settlement, and resort to regional agencies or arrangements, or other peaceful means of their own choice.*

2. The Security Council shall, when it deems necessary, call upon the parties to settle their dispute by such means.

This Article 33 stipulated the parties must seek a peaceful resolution by negotiation, enquiry and to resort to regional agencies or arrangements and other peaceful means of their own choice. Shelem Ministry stated in Part 1 of the Madad the Palestinian Arabs and the Israeli must restore the everlasting covenant of peace which includes the ancient landmarks given to Shem, Abraham and Mosheh for settling his children in their allotted inheritance. The 1967 armistice lands were never recognized by any nations as permanent borders but only cease fire boundary lines for the establishment of peace negotiations between the Arabs and Israelis. The United Nations resolutions 242 to which all existing resolution have been based on has at its core the 1967 armistice lines that were never permanent borders for the Palestinians nor the Israelis. Notice this fact is validated by the chief author of United Nations Resolution 242 **Hugh Mackintosh Foot, Baron Caradon also known as Lord Caradon:**

ord Caradon, chief author of the resolution, takes a subtly different slant. His focus seems to be that the lack of a definite article is intended to deny permanence to the "unsatisfactory" pre-1967 border, rather than to allow Israel to retain land taken by force. Such a view would appear to allow for the possibility that the borders could be varied through negotiation:

Knowing as I did the unsatisfactory nature of the 1967 line I was not prepared to use wording in the Resolution which would have made that line permanent. Nevertheless it is necessary to say again that the overriding principle was the "inadmissibility of the acquisition of territory by war" and that meant that there could be no justification for annexation of territory on the Arab side of the 1967 line merely because it had been conquered in the 1967 war. The sensible way to decide permanent "secure and recognized" boundaries would be to set up a Boundary Commission and hear both sides and then to make impartial recommendations for a new frontier line, bearing in mind, of course, the "inadmissibility" principle. The purpose is perfectly clear, the principle is stated in the preamble, and the necessity for withdrawal is stated in the operative section. And then the essential phrase which is not sufficiently recognized is that withdrawal should take place to secure and recognized boundaries, and these words were very carefully chosen: they have to be secure and they have to be recognized. They will not be secure unless they are recognized. And that is why one has to work for agreement. This is essential. I would defend absolutely what we did. It was not for us to lay down exactly where the border should be. I know the 1967 border very well. It is not a satisfactory border, it is where troops had to stop in 1948, just where they happened to be that night that is not a permanent boundary... *(From Wikipedia, UNSC Resolution 242.)*

This resolution takes into consideration the admissibility principle but it does not reflect on the conquest of the land of the Hebrews by several nations from the beginning. The United Nations has the opportunity in this generations to correct years of illegal occupation in the name of conquest and the progression of the colonist ambitions for world dominance. The land that is now the center of years of controversy is one that has been envied, coveted and occupied illegal by many nations. This land must revert back to the people who it was divinely appointed by an everlasting covenant of peace. The boundary lines and borders within this inheritance must reflect those outline in the Holy Writ for both Hebrew and the Arabs. The reality of this undertaken to restore these ancient landmarks can be seen in the Israel-Egypt Peace Treaty of 1979 and the Israel-Jordan Treaty of Peace in 1994, that established the Jordan River as the boundary of Jordan.

The negotiation must be based on the ancient landmarks given to Shem, Abraham and Mosheh outlined in the Holy Writ. This boundaries lines and borders will secure for the children of Abraham their allotted inheritance. The Hebrews and Arabs must adopt the laws concerning the treatment of strangers in their lands and allot to the strangers a certain amount of inherited land within their respectful lands. The re-establishment of these ancient borders would solve the issues impeding peace in the Middle East today. This would solve the security needs of Israelis and establish the two-state solution outlined in the Arab Peace Initiative and the United Nations resolutions to end the Israeli and the Palestinian conflict. These boundary lines and borders must be agreed upon by all nations in the region by a regional agreement for the establishment of these ancient borders. The Palestinians will have two options to migrate into the allotted lands establish by Abraham their orefather and the other option is to exercise a right given them in the laws of peace. The children of Israel once the land is divided again as inheritance to the 12 tribes are commanded to allot a portion of land as an inheritance for the stranger among them.

So shall ye divide this land unto you according to the tribes of Israel? And it shall come to pass, *that* you shall divide it by lot for an inheritance unto you, and to the strangers that sojourn among you, which shall beget children among you: and they shall be unto you as born in the country among the children of Israel; they shall have inheritance with you among the tribes of Israel. And it shall come to pass, *that* in what tribe the stranger sojourns, there shall you give *him* his inheritance, says Father Yahweh.

Ezekiel 47:21-23 (KJV)

The prophet Yechetzqyah (Ezekiel) gives us the boundary lines and borders that Yahweh predicted and commanded to be re-establish in Ezekiel 47:13-23 and Ezekiel 48:1-29. These borders must be agreed upon by all the regional Arab nations for the establishment of lasting peace. The re-establishment of the ancient landmark will bring about the two state solution were the Palestinians can have their own homeland.

The former Prime Minister of Israel Ehud Barak in a speech recently acknowledging the right of Israelites to the land, but he cast doubt concerning the ancient boundary lines establish by an everlasting covenant of peace. He stated in his speech the ancient borders change frequently throughout the occupation of the land by the children of Israel. He recounted the days of King David and the Second Temple were he stated the borders moved like an "accordion". Mr. Barak has failed to realize the borders on which he stated moved like an accordion were still within the boundary lines of the divinely appointed land promise to Arphaxad, Abraham, Isaac and Yaaqob. The borders only moved because Esau the progenitor of Edom and Lot the progenitor of Ammonites, and the Moabites and the Philistines descendants from the patriarch Pathrusim rose up against the children of Israel. Yahweh as result of their hostility toward the children of Israel gave them their allotted inheritance of land to possess.

Yahweh spoke to me, saying, you are to pass over through Ar, the coast of Moab, this day: And *when* you come close to the children of Ammon, distress them not, nor meddle with them: **_for I will not give you of the land of the children of Ammon as an possession_**; because I have given it unto the children of Lot *for* a possession. (That also was accounted a land of giants: giants dwelt therein in old time; and the Ammonites call them Zamzummims; A people great, and many, and tall, as the Anakims; but Yahweh destroyed them before them; and they succeeded them, and dwelt in their stead: As he did to the children of Esau, which dwelt in Seir, when he destroyed the Horims from before them; and they succeeded them, and dwelt in their stead even unto this day: And the Avims which dwelt in Hazerim, *even* unto Azzah, the Caphtorims, which came forth out of Caphtor, destroyed them, and dwelt in their stead.)

Deuteronomy 2:17-23 (KJV)

And Jephthah sent messengers again unto the king of the children of Ammon: And said unto him, This what Jephthah says, Israel took not away the land of Moab, nor the land of the children of Ammon: But when Israel came up from Egypt, and walked through the wilderness unto the Red sea, and came to Kadesh; Then Israel sent messengers unto the king of Edom, saying, Let me, I pray, pass through your land: but the king of Edom would not hearken *thereto.* And in like manner they sent into the king of Moab: but he would not *consent*: and Israel remained in Kadesh. Then they went along through the wilderness, and compassed the land of Edom, and the land of Moab, and came by the east side of the land of Moab, and pitched on the other side of Arnon, but came not within the border of Moab: for Arnon was the border of Moab. Israel sent messengers unto Sihon king of the Amorites, the king of Heshbon; and Israel said unto him, Let us pass, we pray, through your land into my place. But Sihon trusted not Israel to pass through his coast: but Sihon gathered all his people together, and pitched in Jahaz, and fought against Israel. Yahweh the Father of Israel delivered Sihon and all his people into the hand of Israel, and they smote them: so Israel possessed all the land of the Amorites, the inhabitants of that country. And they possessed all the coasts of the Amorites, from Arnon even unto Jabbok, and from the wilderness even unto Jordan.

Judges 11:14-22 (KJV)

The former Prime Minister of Israel Ehud Barak also stated in his speech about the physical borders to which a political nation fulfills its right is different from the divinely appointed borders within ancient Israel. He said the physical borders are determined by a geostrategic reality and not by ancient landmarks establish in days of old. The question we have for Mr. Barak are any other political leader who shares his view are the geostrategic borders he is speaking of the 1967 armistice lines stipulated in UN resolution 242? If these are the physical borders he is referring to it is a known fact from the commencement of this resolution "confusion" set in concerning wither the Israeli government should withdraw from all or some of the occupy territory. The armistice lines of 1967 are not recognized today as permanent borders to be consider for lasting peace to be establish in land. The armistice lines and territory within it are considered by the community of nations to be occupied territory. This is a hypocritical conviction held by the nations and it does not take into considerations prior occupation of the land of Israel that were clearly accomplish by conquest. The question we ask the community of nation does the admissibility principle apply to previous occupation by the Arab nations who claim title to the land by conquest? We must be honest with ourselves and stand for true justice and peace for if we continue to be partial in any regards to these issue we will never experience the lasting peace we all hope for.

The other pressing issue impeding the establishment of peace is the Palestinians refusing to recognize Israel as Jewish Nation. Shelem Ministry admonish the nations to really examine the reason why the Palestinians refuse to recognize a Jewish State. The Palestinian leaders concerns in regard to this issue should not be ignore and their concerns should not be view as illegitimate are hateful. There concerns and views in regards to this issues need to be examine and investigated to establish wither they are validate are not. The Zionist Movement was viewed by the Palestinian Arabs and all Arabs nations as a movement for the complete dispossession of the indigenous Arab population so a Jewish state could be establish. This movement posed a threat to the very existence of the Arabs in the land. History has recorded for us the Arabs have occupied the land since the seventh century A.D. this is over 1200 years but the fact remains this was by conquest. The Arabs believed that Zionism was based on a colonialist worldview and the dispossession of their people from the land. It is a known historical fact the Zionist were a distinct minority of the Jewish people in Europe until after WWII. This minority within the Jewish communities throughout Europe saw their economic and social lifestyles being challenged and declining within all European nations. They began to seek a place where Jews could master their own fate. The inspiration was stemmed from a group of Grecians who sought to be reestablish in their homeland of Greece. This small minority of Zionist began to see European Jewry coming to end this began to materialize in the 1930's. The actions of the Zionist was motivated by desperation and survival they began seek a homeland for the Jews who resided throughout Europe. The Zionist movement was perceived by the Arabs nations as threat after they began to see the Zionist claiming Palestine as the rightful possession of the Jewish People while advocating the exclusion of its Arab inhabitants. This ideology has caused the continued present of war and fighting between these two people. The Arabs are also by an everlasting covenant of peace rightful inheritors of the land given to Abraham their forefather. The children of Abraham stemming from Ishmael and Keturah who make up the Arab Nations today inherited the east country adjacent to the inheritance of Isaac. We discussed in detail this inheritance in part one of the Madad and how this land was assigned to the Arabs by an everlasting covenant of peace. The Arabs residing within the inheritance of children of Israel are to be given as an inheritance land and to be treated as a native born.

In 1907 an article written by Yitzhak Epstein in Hashiloah called for a new Zionist policy which he laid out a solution to the exclusion policy of the Zionist. Mr. Epstein solution were in unity with the provision described in the laws of peace given to Mosheh in regard to the treatment of a stranger. He desired to create a binational, nonexclusive program for the settlement and development of land. He desire to create a joint community consisted of Arabs and Hebrews farming communities. He desired to create schools, hospitals and libraries that would be non-exclusive and the education bilingual for strengthening cooperation between both Arabs and Jews.

The reality of these two people leaving side by side in peace can never be a reality if long held beliefs and ideologies persist. The Partition Plan of United Nations was rejected by the Arabs because it establish the Jews as the ruling body. These would not be the case if both Arabs and Hebrews reestablish the "covenant of peace" made with Abraham their forefather. This covenant consist of a body of laws that would reestablish the brotherhood, faith, and cooperation once shared by these brothers.

The negotiation to end the conflict in the land can never be realize if the Zionist ideologies continue to create an atmosphere of distrust among the Arabs. The Zionist leader by the name of David Ben-Gurion had begun to proposal to the Zionist "we shall abolish the partition plan and expand into the whole of Palestine". This was followed in 1948 by Menachem Begin who declared the partition of the homeland illegal and he advocated the partition plan was invalid. The Israeli government used their superior military preparation and organization to occupy by force the cities inhabited by many Arabs.

The policy of the Zionist organization of expansionism which Ben-Gurion's advocated were based on what was term practical considerations on the restoration of Biblical borders as the borders of the Jewish State. The political aspiration to restore these borders were never consider to be part of the negotiation but the means they chose to achieved their end occupation by military force has impeded the establishment of lasting peace in the Middle East.

In the Israeli Prime Minister Moshe Sharatt's personal diaries there was found an excerpt from May of 1955 which he quotes Moshe Dayan as following: *"Israel must see the sword as the main, if not the only, instrument to keep its morale high and to retain its moral tension toward this end. We must invent dangers, and to do this it must adopt the method of provocation-and-revenge.... And above all let us hope for a ew war with the Arab counties, so that we may finally get rid of our* *roubles and acquire our space."* **Quoted in Livia Rokach, "Israel's Sacred** *"errorism".***

The above ideologies and policy of that time caused the deep seated enmity and hatred toward the Zionist organization. The long held beliefs with their provocative means have fostered a state of distrust and the unwillingness of the Palestinian Arabs to negotiate a peace agreement with the Israeli government. This important question remains to be answered by the world body of nations. If both the Jews and Arabs claimed the land to be their possession and both claim the other right to the land to be illegitimate. Then would it not be practical to return to a time in mankind's history when the earth was divided to all nations as an inheritance by an everlasting covenant to solve the issues concerning the borders, *the inadmissibility of the acquisition of territory by war* and conquest and to establish each of these nations in their respectful territory assigned by the covenant of peace? These issue can be resolved only by restoring and adhering to the everlasting covenant of peace. A covenant that both Hebrews and Arab entered into through their common ancestor Abraham. The borders, the provisions concerning migration into assigned territory and the right of inheritance are all covered in this covenant.

The provision within the covenant of peace concerning the treatment of strangers in assigned territory would reestablish trust in the Palestinian people who have been severely oppressed and mistreat by the ruling government in violation of the laws of peace. Shelem Ministry strongly believes if the government of Israel would change its stance and ensure the Palestinian people they would not be mistreated nor oppressed. And if Israel would follow and return to the laws of peace outline in the Holy

Writ then and only then would there be peace. The ideology advocated by Joseph Weitz who wrote the following: _It must be clear that there is no room for both people in this country... The Zionist enterprise so far... Has been fine and good in its own time and could do with land buying but this will not bring about the State of Israel. This must come all at once in the manner of a Salvation and there is no way besides transferring the Arabs from here to the neighboring countries, to transfer them all we cannot leave a single village or a single tribe._ **Quoted from "The Question of Palestine".**

These are the wounds inflicted upon a people that remain as a hindrance for establishing lasting peace. These wounds must be healed by changing the perception of and appearance of any of these ideologies from the minds of the leaders of Palestinian people, and to heal also the physiological wounds it has inflicted on the Palestinian people. The laws of peace we presented in Part I of the Madad concerning the rights of the stranger will put an end to years of injustice and the conflicts that have impeded the establishment of lasting peace in land. The United Nation Resolution 194 supports the provisions outline in the laws of peace concerning the rights of strangers: the UN Resolution calls for the moral and political right of a person or people to return to his place of uninterrupted residence and for a Palestinian Arab to return be compensated for his property and live in Israel as a citizen equal before the law with a Jewish Israeli. Notice the following provision outline in the Holy Writ:

One ordinance _shall be both_ for you of the congregation, and also for the stranger that sojourns _with you_, an ordinance forever in your generations: as you _are_, so shall the stranger be before Yahweh. One law and one manner shall be for you, and for the stranger that sojourns with you.

Number 15:15-16 (KJV)

He execute the judgment of the fatherless and widow, and loves the stranger, giving him food and raiment. Love you therefore the stranger: for you were strangers in the land of Egypt.

Deuteronomy 10:18-19 (KJV)

So shall you divide this land unto you according to the tribes of Israel it shall come to pass, *that* you shall divide it by lot for an inheritance unto you, and to the strangers that sojourn among you, which shall beget children among you: and they shall be unto you as born in the country among the children of Israel; they shall have an inheritance with you among the tribes of Israel. And it shall come to pass, *that* in whatever tribe the stranger sojourns, there shall you give *him* his inheritance, says Father Yahweh.

Ezekiel 47:21-23 (KJV)

The government of Israel must return to the laws of peace and renew the everlasting covenant of peace. The laws of peace concerning the rights of the stranger would solve the issues that caused the negotiations to fail after the 1948-1949 wars, and also all the negotiation that have until this day failed to establish lasting peace.

There is one more issue we must address concerning the Palestinian leaders unwillingness to recognized Jewish State. This argument was recently reiterate in a speech given by an PLO Ambassador to Chile Imad Nabil Jada'a notice this in the following information:

The Jewish people does not exist, PLO Ambassador to Chile Imad Nabil Jada'a told an audience during a talk he gave in Santiago this May, according to a video released by the Institute for the Study of Global

Anti-Semitism and Policy.

Addressing members of the "Gran Logia" Masonic Lodge, Jada'a said that Palestinians "don't recognize the existence of the Jewish people" as there is not, in fact, any such people.

"This is not my personal analysis. Here we can refer to the Jewish Israeli professor from the University of Tel Aviv, Dr. Shlomo Sand, in his book 'The Invention of the Jewish People.' A Jew with Israeli passport announces that, the so-called Jewish nation is a made up invention. Because a religion cannot be a people," he said.

"The Protocols of the Elders of Zion" PLO Ambassador to Chile, Mr. Imad Nabil Jada'a from ISGAP on Vimeo.

Sand believes that contemporary Jews are descended from the Khazar people from the Caucasus and are not connected to the Biblical Israelites. His ideas are widely opposed both in academia and among Jews.

"Until 1896 when a group of academic intellectuals, financial advisers, majority being non-Jewish Europeans, decided to create the Zionist movement with one pretext/excuse; the creation of a homeland for the Jewish people. Although the truth is that this (the goal) is to protect their plans of dominating life in the entire planet," he added.

Jada'a also recommended that his listeners read the The Protocols of the Elders of Zion, a Czarist forgery published in the early 20th century purporting to expose the inner workings of a global Jewish conspiracy.

We know from history that anti-Semitism begins with Jews but never ends with Jews," said Dr. Charles Small, the director of ISGAP.

"For too long Palestinian and western leaders have been tolerating the intolerable i.e. Incitement to genocidal anti-Semitism as prescribed by the Muslim brotherhood, some Palestinian leadership and other Islamists. Tolerating the intolerable social movements is leading to carnage throughout the region. It's time for responsible leaders to put an end to this spreading disease of hatred at the regional level and at the international levels. *Article taken from the Jerusalem Post*

This is an issue needing to be address and the Palestinian leaders should not be held by the government of Israel as Anti-Semitic but the issues should be settled peacefully. Shelem Ministry cannot get into the specifics concerning this issues in this particular work but will write in a separate work about some of the issue stated above. The above speech was not the first time in history this argument has been address. There is some truth to the statement made above and United Nations must investigate the validity of the some of the statement made above. The Egyptian Premier Gamal Abdel Nasser made a similar statement when he was asked about peace in the middle east after their war with Israel he was quoted as saying: *"The Jews will never be able to live her in peace because they left here black but the came back white." Quote taken from "Time Magazine"*

The Arab Nations have held this belief for many years and contested the claim of the European Jews claim to be the biblical Israelites who original occupied the land of Israel. The issue can be easily address and resolved by simply acknowledging the facts of history and not denying the truth concerning this issue. The Israeli governments has opportunity in this generation to fulfill prophecy and restore to the land children of Israel who remain scattered throughout the nations. We will explain the specific of this opportunity in a future work and how returning the exiled and the original Hebrew/Israelites spoken of in the bible will remove the obstacles preventing lasting peace to be establish in the Middle East.

The above information needs to be considered by both Israelis and Palestinians when they began to negotiate on solution for peace. Shelem Ministry presents the information to help in the negotiation process for the two-state solution and the ending of years of war and fighting. The Israeli's and the Palestinians have an opportunity to bring to pass an historical event and honor their common ancestor by restoring the covenant made with him and his descendants. This everlasting covenant of peace identifies both the Arabs and the Hebrews as lawful inheritors of the land establishing for each their respectful borders and boundary lines securing for them a perpetual right of inheritance. The United Nations principle concerning the "inadmissibility of the acquisition of territory by war or conquest needs to address the Arab Conquest and the history concerning the land of Israel being occupied by many nations. The United Nations can reverse the injustice and restore the original people who by right of inheritance received this land by divine appointment from Yahweh our Heavenly Father. This generation has an opportunity to restore once again the work of the Madad the stretching forth of the measuring line to restore the ancient landmarks in the holy land. We have at this time the opportunity to reverse years of injustice and finally stablish peace in the Middle East. We leave you with this inspiring scripture in the Holy Writ:

These *are* the things that ye shall do; Speak ye every man the truth to his neighbor; execute the judgment of truth and peace in your gates: And let none of you imagine evil in your hearts against his neighbor; and do not love to vow false oath: for all these *things* I hate, says Yahweh.

Zechariah 8:16-17 (KJV)

Therefore, love truth and peace.

Zechariah 8:19 (KJV)

A generous open-hearted and Princely man writes on all his possession for myself and for mankind.

www.ingramcontent.com/pod-product-compliance
Lightning Source LLC
Chambersburg PA
CBHW051141250726
48655CB00007B/3178